30 PAPER CREATIONS

Fantastic papercraft projects to make

ULTIMATE
EDITIONS

No pastime is safer than papercraft, but you should remember the following points:

Always choose non-toxic materials whenever possible; for example PVA (white glue), strong clear glue and non-toxic poster paints.

Children love papercrafts, but should only be allowed to use sharp tools under supervision.

Always use a cutting board or cutting mat to avoid damage to household surfaces (it is also safer to cut on a hard surface).

Protect surfaces from paint and glue splashes by laying down old newspapers.

First published in 1996 by Ultimate Editions

© 1996 Anness Publishing Limited

Ultimate Editions is an imprint of
Anness Publishing Limited
Boundary Row Studios
1 Boundary Row
London SE1 8HP

ISBN 1 86035 191 3

Distributed in Canada by Book Express, an imprint of
Raincoast Books Distribution Limited

Publisher: Joanna Lorenz
Project Editor: Fiona Eaton
Designer: Lilian Lindblom
Illustrations: Anna Koska, Lorraine Harrison
Contributors: Angela A'Court, Marion Elliot
Photographer: Martin Norris
Jacket Photographer: Amanda Heywood

Printed and bound in China

CONTENTS

INTRODUCTION

Paper is everywhere: our lives would be impossible without wrappings, letters, magazines, cards, packaging, leaflets, posters, newspapers and notepads. It is one of the most inexpensive and readily available materials, yet it is commonly neglected as a craft, art and hobby medium. With the help of this book, and a little imagination and enthusiasm, you can learn to transform this simple, functional and cost-effective material into fantastic personalized gifts, wonderful shapes, delightful stationery and beautiful objects, such as mobiles, boxes, lampshades and decorations.

CLASSIC LINES

If you want to write a letter in a hurry, but still want it to be stylish,
here are a couple of quick ways to make some beautiful writing paper.
You will need some light-coloured wrapping paper in a classical design.

MATERIALS

scissors
pale wrapping paper
tracing paper
glue
sheet of white paper

1 Cut out a rectangle of wrapping paper to the size of the writing paper, and cut a piece of tracing paper the same size. Stick the tracing paper on top of the wrapping paper, smoothing out any bubbles. Use a black felt-tip pen to write your letter so that it shows up clearly.

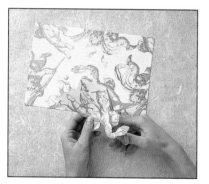

2 If you have a bit more time you could select a motif from the wrapping paper and cut this out.

3 Glue the motif to a sheet of white paper.

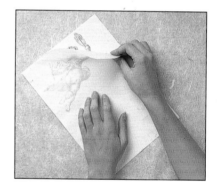

4 As before, glue a sheet of tracing paper on top to give an elegant double layer. You could make a collection of writing paper by cutting out different motifs from one sheet of wrapping paper.

COLLAGE TAGS

When you want to keep things simple and have perhaps used a plain paper
to wrap your present, a collaged gift tag can be the perfect finishing touch.
They can be as easy or as complicated as you want to make them.

MATERIALS

scissors
green paper
glue
orange card
hole punch
coloured thread or ribbon

1 For the Grecian-style tag cut out a Grecian urn and decorative dots in green paper.

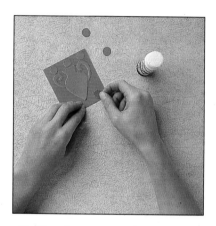

2 Glue them on to a folded piece of orange card.

3 Punch a hole and thread through a length of coloured thread or ribbon.

CUT-AND-THREAD PAPER

Make plain writing paper extra special with simple strips of crêpe paper threaded through in unusual patterns. Practise first on spare paper to get the right effect.

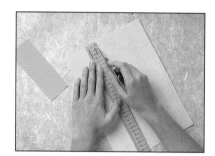

1 Take a sheet of writing paper and mark two sets of two vertical lines at the top, in the centre. The lines should be approximately 2 cm (¾ in) long and 2.5 cm (1 in) apart. Cut through the lines using a craft knife.

2 Cut a piece of crêpe paper in a toning colour to your writing paper. Thread it under the "bridges" taking care not to break them.

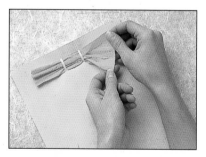

3 Once the crêpe paper is centred, arrange the bow by fanning out the sides.

4 Repeat the bow design on the extended back flap of an envelope to complete the writing set.

5 Another effect can be achieved by marking and cutting out a series of vertical lines across the top of the page. Cut a piece of crêpe paper into a strip the same width as the slots, and a thinner strip in a stronger colour.

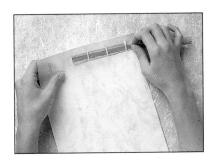

6 Fold the paper in half to thread the strips through easily, and then open up.

7 Instead of using vertical lines, this version uses two staggered lines of horizontal slits. Once again, thread the strip of crêpe paper through and see the diagonal pattern it makes.

21st Birthday Pop-up

This unusual card is perfect for celebrating a special birthday. Once you have mastered the simple pop-up technique you could use different numbers for a variety of important birthdays.

MATERIALS

pencil
plain paper
stiff white paper
craft knife
poster paints and paintbrush
glue
stiff coloured paper

1 Scale up the "21" shape to the size required and transfer to a piece of stiff white paper. Cut it out using a craft knife and paint the numbers. When the paint is dry, fold the "21" shape in half and glue the underside of each tab.

2 Next, fold a piece of stiff coloured paper in two to form a card shape. Glue one tab to one half of the backing card, so that the bottom of the crease down the middle of the "21" exactly touches the crease on the card.

3 To finish off, apply glue to the second tab and fold the empty half of the backing card over the top of the second tab. When unfolded, the card will stick to this second tab, pulling up the "21". Decorate the base card.

WRAPPING A SPHERE

A sphere-shaped present is always a difficult shape to wrap up and it can be approached in two ways. The gift can either be placed in the centre of a piece of paper which can then be gathered up into a bunch above the present and tied with ribbon, or the paper can be pleated, as here.

MATERIALS

sphere-shaped present
wrapping paper
scissors
sticky tape
double-sided tape

1 Place the present in the centre of a square piece of wrapping paper. Make the square into a circle by rounding off the corners.

2 Start by bringing one section of the paper up to the top. Now work around the circle by pleating the paper so that it hugs the shape of the sphere. Use sticky tape to secure the pleats as you go round.

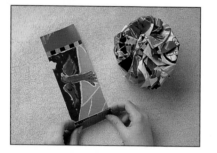

3 Continue to pleat neatly until you have gone all the way around. To finish, make a pleated fan. Fold a strip of paper in half with the right side outside. Pleat the paper along its length.

4 Then, pinch the pleats together at the bottom and fan out the sides. Attach it to the present by fixing with double-sided tape.

TAG TIME

Make your own gift tags for a personal touch as well as to save money.
Used greetings cards can often be cut down and made into brand-new gift
tags. Another idea is to take a motif from the wrapping paper used
to cover your present.

MATERIALS

scissors
wrapping paper or greetings cards
glue
thin card
ribbon

1 When you have wrapped the present, cut out a suitable motif from the spare paper. Glue the motif on to some thin card in a co-ordinating colour.

2 Following the shape of the motif, cut around the design so that the card forms a border.

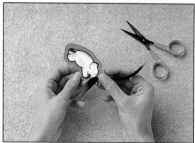

3 Now punch a hole in the card with a scissor blade and thread a ribbon through the hole. Write a message on the tag and attach it to the present.

STAND-UP PLACE NAMES

Make your place cards really stand out with these novelty motifs that project above the cards.

MATERIALS

green, orange, red and white card
scissors
glue
gold metallic pen
craft knife

1 Fold a square of green card in half. Cut out an octopus from the orange card and position it so the top half is above the fold line. Cut out the facial features from the green card and glue in place.

2 For a festive place name, cut out two holly leaves in green. Stick them on to the top of a red place card so that the holly is sticking upwards. Cut out and glue on red dots for the berries.

3 To make the rocket, mark the fold line on the card and lay it flat. Draw the rocket with gold pen so that the top extends over the fold line. With a craft knife, cut around the top part only. Then fold the card and the rocket will stand up.

SECRET MESSAGES

Give a sense of mystery to your gifts by adding a tag tied with a ribbon bow to conceal your message. A perfect idea for sending notes to loved ones.

coloured card
craft knife
ruler
contrasting coloured paper
gold metallic pen
glue
gold ribbon

1 Take a rectangle of card and fold in half. Open out the card and make a small narrow slit for the ribbon on the centre of both leading edges, back and front.

2 On a separate piece of contrasting paper draw a design with a gold pen and stick this on to the card.

3 Write your message inside and then thread a length of gold ribbon through the slits and tie a bow to keep the wording a secret.

Candy Cones

Pretty and simple ideas for arranging candies at a wedding or party. For an alternative, wrap a red ribbon upwards around a cone made from elegant wrapping paper and use matching red tissue paper inside.

MATERIALS

20 cm (8 in) square of wrapping paper
glue
rosette
tissue paper
sugared almonds or candies

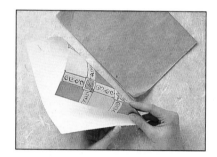

1 Roll the square of wrapping paper into a cone, starting with a corner and shaping it into a rounded form.

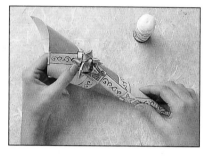

2 Glue the cone together along the edge and stick a rosette on the overlapping point. Flatten the cone at the closed end.

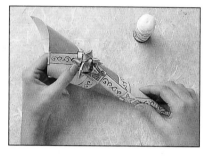

3 Scrunch up some matching tissue paper and push this into the open end. Fill with sugared almonds or candies.

You can vary the design of the cones, depending on the occasion, using different paper and ribbons.

MATERIALS

scissors
black and gold paper
pencil
glue
ribbon or bow
tissue paper
chocolate coins

1 For a variation, cut one square in black paper and another in gold paper. Zigzag the edges along two adjacent sides of the black square, first drawing a line about 1.5 cm (¾ in) from the edge as a guideline.

2 Then glue the black paper on to the gold paper and roll up into a cone form, gluing along the edges where they overlap.

3 Slightly flatten the end of the cone and stick on a bow or pieces of ribbon.

4 Take some contrasting tissue paper and scrunch it up and insert it into the cone. Fill with chocolate coins.

GIFT BAG

This gift bag is simple to make and adds a touch of elegance to any present. It can be used instead of separate wrapping paper and is sturdy enough to hold a variety of gifts.

MATERIALS

pencil
paper
ruler
decorated paper
craft knife
glue
hole punch
scissors
ribbon

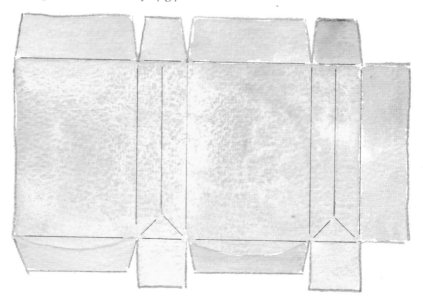

1 Scale up the template using pencil, paper and a ruler to the size required and transfer the pattern on to the decorated paper. Cut out carefully using a craft knife. Score lightly along the back of the creases so that they will fold more easily. Fold down and glue the flaps along the top edge of the bag.

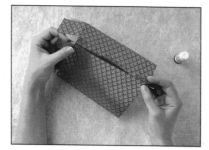

2 Next, glue the long side tab to form the bag shape.

3 Then glue the base of the bag in position, folding in the short end tabs first.

4 Form the pleats down the sides of the bag by pressing the long edges together gently so that the paper is pushed inwards.

5 Using the hole punch, make two holes on each of the top sides near the upper edge. Cut two short lengths of ribbon and thread each end through the holes to make two looped handles. Knot the ends at the back of the holes to secure.

STENCIL STYLE

Use ready-made stencils or cut your own to make this stylish writing paper.
Dab on stencil paints or colour with soft crayons for speedy results.

MATERIALS

pencil
stencilling card
craft knife
paint
saucer
stencil brush
writing paper
crayon

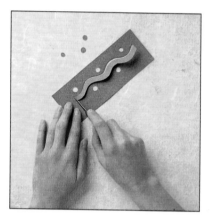

1 Using the template and a pencil, transfer the motif on to stencilling card in the size you need and cut out using a craft knife.

2 Prepare the paint on a saucer and collect the colour on to a stencil brush. Then, holding the stencilling card firmly, dab the brush on to the writing paper using a circular movement.

3 Instead of using paint, a coloured crayon could be used. Once again, hold the stencilling card firmly and lightly fill in the pattern, remembering to work all the crayon strokes in the same direction for a neat finish.

PAPER QUILLS

The old-fashioned papercraft known as quilling is used to make this distinctive card. You can design a picture in the same way, and hang it on the wall.

MATERIALS

*scissors
assorted coloured papers
strong clear glue
contrasting coloured card*

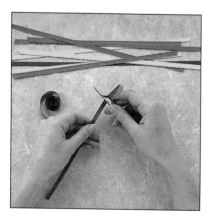

1 Cut long narrow strips of various shades of coloured paper. First curl one end of each strip with the blunt edge of a pair of scissors, then, starting at this end, roll the strip into a tight coil.

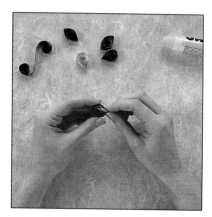

2 Release the coil slightly and glue the end. Hold this in position until the glue is dry. Pinch the outside of the coils between your fingers to form different shapes such as a pear, scroll or eye.

3 Fold a rectangular piece of card in a contrasting colour in half. Arrange the shaped quills on the card and stick down, spreading the glue on the bottom edge of each quill.

BEAUTIFUL BINDING

If you have an old book or album which you want to brighten up, you can learn how to cover your own pages. For this project you will need to determine the size of your book.

MATERIALS

ruler
craft knife
book or photograph album
thick card
adhesive cloth tape
glue
patterned and plain wrapping paper
pencil
hole punch
cord

1 First cut two pieces of thick card that are about 1 cm (½ in) wider and longer than the pages to be covered. If you are covering a loose-leaf album, measure the side strip of the album sheet which has the holes punched in it, and mark the same amount on to the top of one of the cards, which will eventually be the top cover. Cut a small strip off one side of this.

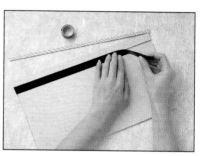

2 Using the other back card as a measure, place the trimmed top card on it and put the narrow strip above so that there is a gap between them where the strip has been removed. Tape the pieces together using adhesive cloth tape. Turn the block over and put another piece of the cloth tape on the other side, thus making the hinge for the top cover.

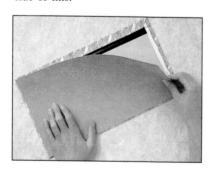

3 Now glue on a sheet of decorative paper to cover the outsides. Glue a toning or contrasting plain colour to cover the inside.

4 Next lay an album or page sheet on to the bottom cover and draw where the holes are on it. Punch them through using a hole punch. Repeat the process with the front cover.

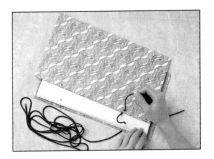

5 Now place the pages on to the back cover so that the holes are aligned and put the front cover on top. To finish off, thread a good quality cord through the holes.

ANTIQUE MARBLING

There are several methods of marbling paper to achieve the beautiful effects seen on old bookbinding and traditional Italian stationery. The process involves suspending pigment on the surface of water, arranging the colour into patterns, and transferring these to paper.

MATERIALS

metal roasting pan or deep tray
cold water
scissors
paper
oil paints in various colours
white spirit
paintbrush or metal skewer

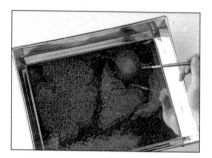

1 Half fill a clean metal roasting pan or a deep tray with cold water. Cut a piece of paper to fit the size of the container. Thin a little oil paint with white spirit, and dot the diluted paint on to the surface of the water with a brush or skewer.

2 The paint will disperse, creating patterns on the surface of the water. Hold the paper by the top right- and bottom left-hand corners and lower it across the surface of the water in a rolling movement.

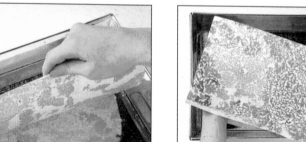

TIP
Before marbling subsequent pieces of paper, skim the surface of the water with scrap paper to pick up excess paint and keep the water clean.

3 Carefully lift the paper from the container. The paint will adhere to the paper, giving a marbled effect. Lay the sheets out to dry at room temperature.

4 To create multi-coloured patterns add more colours to the water. Use a paintbrush or metal skewer to move the colours around before laying down the paper.

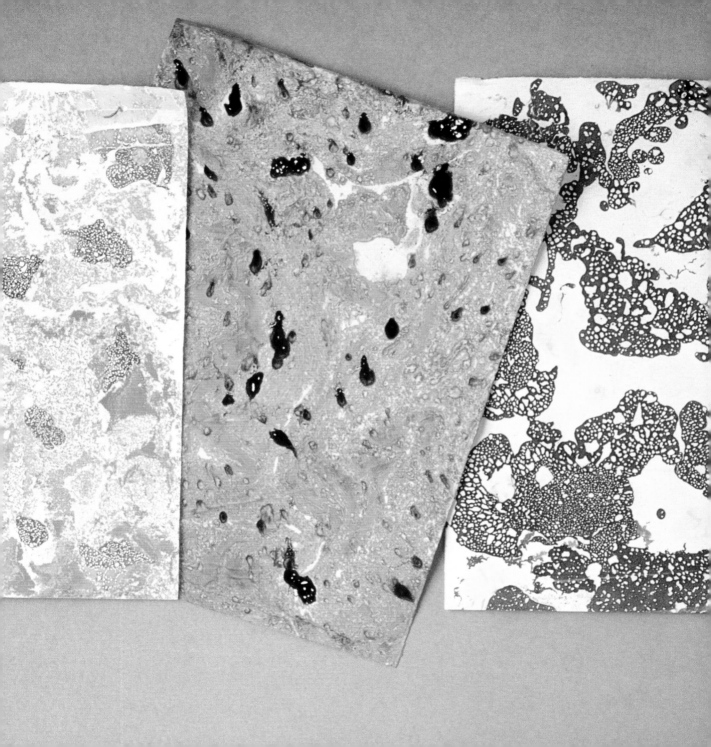

ONE-PIECE GIFT BOXES

This box is constructed from a single piece of card and can be closed tightly, making it an ideal container, either vertical or horizontal, for candies or small biscuits.

MATERIALS

pencil
thin card
craft knife
glue

1 Scale up the template to the size required, and transfer it to the card. Cut it out using a craft knife. Score along the back folds of the tabs. Fold up the sides of the box and glue the end tab to make a tube shape.

2 Interlock the tabs at the base of the box; it should lock securely without the use of glue.

VALENTINE'S HEART

This pop-up surprise will add a touch of fun to Valentine's Day. The same technique can be used to make cards for other occasions, such as a tree for Christmas time, or a house for a friend's moving day.

MATERIALS

pencil
scissors
stiff paper in red and cream
glue
red felt-tip pen

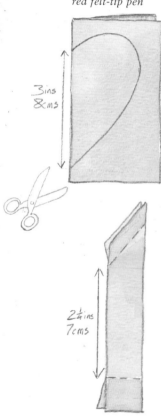

1 Scale up the support from the template to the required size and cut out of a piece of stiff paper. Then fold a matching piece of paper into two halves to form a card. Fold the support to the correct shape, creasing the tabs upwards.

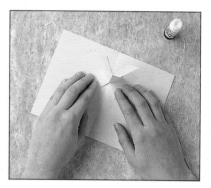

2 Next, glue the support to the backing card near the top, ensuring that the crease on the support exactly touches the crease on the card. Note that the support is symmetrically placed over the crease.

3 Cut out a heart shape in red paper and glue it to the tabs at the top of the support. Decorate the inside border of the card to match with the felt-tip pen. When the card is opened the heart will spring out, giving the recipient a lovely surprise!

NOTELET HOLDER

Take an ordinary writing pad and envelopes and dress them up
in a special notelet holder. All kinds of versions are possible,
made from decorative papers and cards.

MATERIALS

writing paper and envelopes
pencil
scissors
card
ruler
glue
brown paper or wrapping paper
gold metallic pen
craft knife
2 paper fasteners
string

1 To make the notelet holder use one of the envelopes to determine the size, and cut a piece of card, measuring the length of the envelope and adding 8 cm (3 in), by three times the height of the envelope plus 8 cm (3 in).

2 Cut out the card with or without the pointed flap according to the finished style that you require.

3 Apply glue to the unmarked side of the cut-out card, and then cover in brown paper, trimming the edges where necessary. Taking a gold pen, draw a design on to the brown paper.

4 On the inside, score along the marked lines with a craft knife and cut the tab lines.

5 To make the notelets, take six sheets of paper from the writing pad and glue a piece of brown paper or wrapping paper on to each sheet. Trim to size.

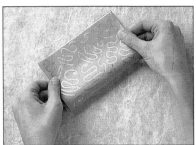

6 Decorate the brown paper with the gold pen as before. Fold the paper in half and pop the six notelets and envelopes into the notelet holder.

7 Fold and glue the holder. Push the fasteners through the flap in the front of the box. Secure the case with a loop of string round each of the fasteners.

CONCENTRIC TWIST

Hang this impressive paper sculpture in a window; if it is made from metallic-coated card it will catch the light as it moves gently in the air currents.

MATERIALS

pencil
thin coloured card
craft knife

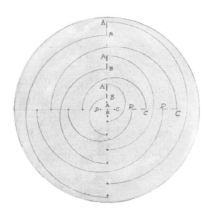

1 Scale up the template to the required size and transfer to coloured card. Cut the slits using a craft knife. Gently twist the central circle away from its frame.

2 Starting at the rim, form the first twist by gently turning the central section at an angle of 90 degrees to the outer ring.

3 Continue to form the twists by turning each ring at the same angle, moving progressively towards the centre, until the twist-out is finally complete.

PERFORMING PIERROT

Children will love to watch the clever movements of this traditional Pierrot puppet. Why not make a couple and put on a show?

MATERIALS

pencil
blue, white and red paper
scissors
black felt-tip pen
glue
4 paper fasteners
metal skewer or scissor blade
thin string
curtain ring

1 Scale up the pieces from the template to the size required and transfer to the coloured paper. Cut out the shapes for the clown: one body, two legs, two arms and a hat in blue; collar, cuffs and pom-poms in white. Mark on reference dots with a black pen. First make up the face by gluing on his hat and rosy cheeks. Draw the face details in with the black felt-tip pen.

2 Glue the pom-poms on to the hat, front and Pierrot's boots, and stick on the collar and cuffs.

3 Match up the dots on the body and the limbs and join them all together by gently pushing the paper fasteners through both layers. Open out the fasteners on the back.

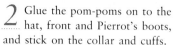

4 On the reverse side, pull the limbs downwards and pierce a hole at the top of each arm using a skewer or scissor blade. Thread a length of thin string through each hole and knot at both ends on the reverse side. Repeat this with the legs to form two "cross bars".

5 Thread a long piece of string through a curtain ring. Attach one end to the centre of the arm string and the other end to the centre of the leg string. Trim if necessary. The strings should not be slack when the limbs are "at rest". When the strings are firmly fixed, pull the ring and watch Pierrot perform.

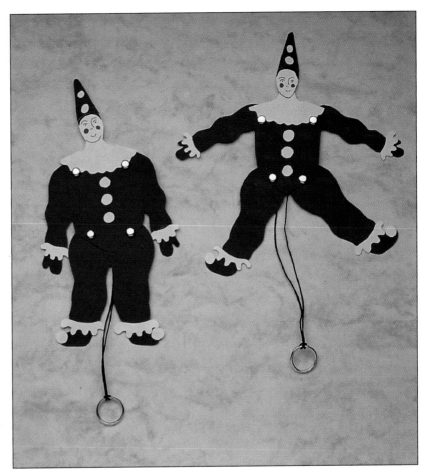

A GREAT CATCH

This handsome fish is displayed proudly on a papier mâché stand, rather
like a trophy. It would be fun to make a papier mâché case displaying
a similar "catch" to hang on the wall!

MATERIALS

pencil
heavy corrugated card
scissors or craft knife
strong clear glue
masking tape
newspaper
diluted PVA (white) glue
fine sandpaper
paintbrush
white paint
poster paints
black ink (optional)
non-toxic clear gloss varnish

1 Scale up the fish shape and stand from the template to the required size, and transfer on to the corrugated card. Cut out two pieces for the stand. Stick the two halves of the stand together with strong clear glue, hold the joins with masking tape and leave to dry.

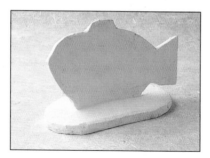

3 Lightly sand down the fish and stand. Prime with white paint.

2 Soak newspaper strips in diluted PVA (white) glue and apply three layers of papier mâché to the fish and stand. Leave them to dry overnight in a warm place.

4 Draw in the fish's face, fins and other features, and then decorate it with poster paints. Use black ink to draw in the detail, if required. Let the fish dry overnight and then seal it with two coats of clear gloss varnish.

POPULAR POPPIES

The stark simplicity of bright red poppies with their black centres
makes them an ideal flower to craft in paper.

MATERIALS

scissors
garden wire
cotton wool (surgical cotton)
green, black and red crêpe paper
sticky tape
glue

1 To make the stem, cut a length of garden wire. Bend the top to make a loop and trap a small amount of cotton wool (surgical cotton) in the loop. Cover this in a cut-out circle of green crêpe paper. Secure by wrapping tape around it.

2 Next cut three small circles of black crêpe paper. Fringe the outer edges and then poke the other end of the wire through the centre and slide up to the green bud.

3 Cut out five petal shapes in red crêpe paper and stretch the outer edges with your fingertips so that they frill.

4 Glue the petals one by one around the base of the centre.

5 Finally, cover the stem in green crêpe paper by winding a long strip around diagonally and securing it at the base with sticky tape.

ELEGANT LAMPSHADE

Add a designed look to your room by using a leftover piece of wallpaper,
or a paper of a complementary colour, to make this lampshade.

MATERIALS

lampshade frame
coloured paper or wallpaper
pen
scissors or craft knife
coin
glue

1 Take a lampshade frame and place it on to your chosen paper. Draw around the shape while slowly moving the frame round to obtain the correct measurement. Now cut out the shape slightly outside the drawn line using scissors or a craft knife to give a piece of paper larger than the frame. Using a coin, draw a scalloped edge along the bottom of the paper.

2 Then cut along it until the edging is complete.

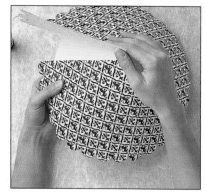

3 Now apply a layer of glue to the frame and carefully attach the paper to it, smoothing it out to avoid bumps or creases.

4 Finally, cut small darts around the top and glue them down, working around until the frame is completely covered and the shade ready to be fitted to a lamp.

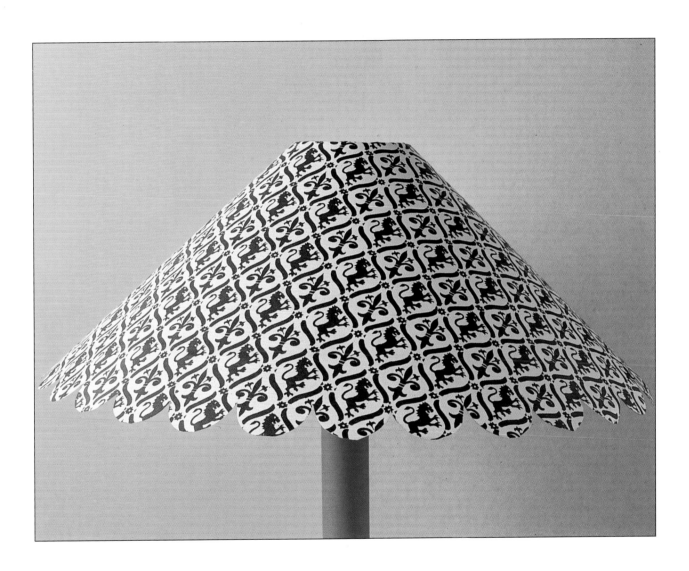

WASTE PAPER BASKET

Découpage decoration quickly covers surfaces in beautiful and unusual designs.
It is particularly effective on shiny materials, such as this metal waste paper basket.

MATERIALS

flat brush
diluted PVA (white) glue
metal waste paper basket
pale blue and yellow tissue paper
scissors
flowery wrapping paper
clear polyurethane varnish

1 Brush dilute PVA (white) glue liberally all over the basket.

2 Tear long strips of tissue paper and paste them round the middle area of the basket.

3 Cut out an assortment of strips and motifs from wrapping paper. Decide on the design of the basket and dip the pieces of wrapping paper in PVA (white) glue. Stick them on to the basket according to your design and brush them flat. Add more strips of the tissue paper until the design is complete. Leave to dry. Finish with a final coat of glue and leave to dry. Finally, cover with a coat of clear polyurethane varnish and leave to dry.

DESIGNER PENCIL POT

This pencil pot is a lovely idea to cheer up your own desk, or it can make a beautiful personalized gift for a friend. The matching pencils add an artistic touch.

MATERIALS

empty cardboard tube or
salt container
tape measure
pencil
scissors
patterned paper
glue

1 First of all you will need to cover the inside of the container. Measure the circumference and height of the pot and cut out two pieces of paper, slightly larger. You could use wallpaper, wrapping paper or marbled paper.

2 Take one of the pieces, glue it and carefully slot it into the inside of the pot, pressing it around the inside walls.

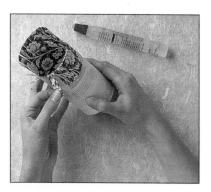

3 Cut darts on the excess paper at the top and glue them down to the outside one by one.

4 Take the other piece of paper and stick it to the outside so that the edge is flush with the top of the pot.

5 Once again cut darts into the excess length at the bottom and glue them on to the base.

6 Now draw around the base of the pot on to the patterned paper and cut out a circle slightly smaller. Glue this and drop it inside the pot and fix to the base.

7 Cut out another circle and glue it to the outside base. To make the matching pencils, cut out a strip of the patterned paper the length of the pencils and approximately three times the width. Glue it and place the pencil at one edge and roll it up. Trim the paper where necessary.

DESK BLOTTER

To make the blotter special it is a good idea to select a wrapping paper to suit the type of desk area. You could choose a hand-made marbled paper for a very traditional look, or an abstract paper or two co-ordinating plain papers for a more modern effect.

MATERIALS

scissors
thick card
patterned paper
glue
thin card
coloured paper
blotting paper

1 Cut a piece of thick card 45 x 30 cm (18 x 12 in). This will be the size of the blotter. Cut your chosen paper 2.5 cm (1 in) larger all round than the card.

2 Next fold and glue the edges of the paper on to the back of the card, mitring the corners by trimming them diagonally.

3 For the corner pieces cut four triangles in thin card measuring 10 x 10 x 14 cm (4 x 4 x 5½ in) and cover them in coloured paper 2.5 cm (1 in) bigger all round. Glue and turn down the bottom edge and the top point. Repeat for all corner pieces.

4 Position the corner pieces on to the corners of the blotter. Turn the board over and fold the edges around, gluing them securely.

5 Cut another piece of coloured paper the same size as the blotter and glue it on to the back. Trim where necessary.

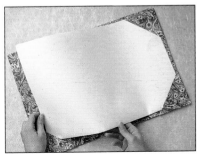

6 Insert a piece of blotting paper under the corners.

TIP
For a co-ordinated desk, why not make the designer pencil pot on pages 50–51 to match the blotter.

SPARKLING FRAME

*This frame is decorated with two different coloured foils, and will take
standard-sized photographs. It opens at the side and could easily be made
larger to accommodate bigger pictures.*

MATERIALS

pencil
heavy corrugated cardboard
thin corrugated cardboard
scissors
strong clear glue
masking tape
diluted PVA (white) glue
2 picture hangers
newspaper
fine sandpaper
paintbrush
white paint
silver foil
gold foil
cord for hanging

1 Scale up the frame pieces from the template to the size you require. Transfer the front to heavy cardboard and the spacer to thin cardboard. Cut a rectangle in heavy cardboard to form the back of the frame. Stick the spacer to three sides of the reverse of this rectangle with strong clear glue and then secure with tape. One side is left open for inserting the picture. When dry, prime the pieces with diluted PVA (white) glue to help prevent warping. Allow to dry for four hours. Glue and tape the hangers to the back.

2 Soak newspaper strips about 2.5 cm (1 in) wide in diluted PVA (white) glue. Cover both pieces of frame with three layers of papier mâché. Let it dry overnight, and then sand the layers lightly with fine sandpaper.

3 Prime the frame pieces with two coats of white paint before they are joined. Although the paint will eventually be covered, you will be able to see much more easily where to stick the foil if the surface of the frame is white. Stick the back to the front of the frame with strong clear glue, and hold the joins together with tape. Cover the joins with two layers of papier mâché strips, and when dry, apply another coat of white paint.

4 To decorate the frame, cut strips of silver foil to fit on the frame and glue them in place. Make sure that you cover the inside edges of the frame. Next, cut shapes from gold foil and stick them around the frame. Finally, attach some cord to the back of the frame, around the hangers.

MONOCHROME DÉCOUPAGE

Découpage is the traditional art of decorating surfaces with paper cut-outs of Victorian-style images. This project has a contemporary feel, however, by using monochrome cut-outs and a modern box covered in brown paper.

MATERIALS

black-and-white pictures
scissors
card or wooden box
glue
varnish (if needed)

1 Start by choosing your images. The ones used here are from wrapping paper. Cut them out carefully following their outlines.

2 Arrange the images on a box and then glue them into position. A card gift box is used here but you could apply the paper cut-outs to a wooden box such as an old cigar box. If you choose a wooden box, you would need to coat the decorated box with a layer of varnish.

TWIRLING PARROTS MOBILE

The movement of these colourful twirling parrots will fascinate young children.

MATERIALS

pencil
tracing paper
thick card
scissors
poster paints
paintbrush
coloured ribbon in 3 colours
dowelling

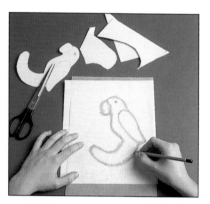

1 Scale up the parrot template to the size required and trace on to thick card. Cut out carefully using scissors. Trace and cut out three parrot shapes.

2 Paint the parrots in a variety of bright colours and leave to dry completely.

3 Pierce a small hole in the back of each parrot's neck and thread through a piece of coloured ribbon. Knot the end to secure and tie the other end to the dowelling. Space the parrots evenly along the dowelling, varying the lengths of ribbon to create a balanced effect. Suspend the mobile by tying a length of ribbon around the centre of the dowelling.

"BAROQUE" CHRISTMAS WREATH

The base for this beautiful wreath is an embroidery hoop. An oval one is used here
but a round one would work just as well.

MATERIALS

scissors
gold crêpe paper
glue
oval embroidery hoop
gold card
paintbrush or pencil
black felt-tip pen

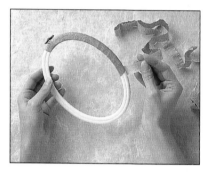

1 Cut a long strip of gold crêpe paper and glue one end to the hoop. Wind the paper around the hoop to cover it completely.

2 Now cut a strip of gold card approximately 1 x 30 cm (½ x 12 in) and wrap it tightly around a paintbrush or pencil.

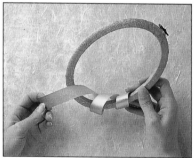

3 Attach one end of the curled gold strip halfway up the right-hand side of the hoop, wind around the hoop and fix the other end just beyond the bottom point.

4 Using the template, scaled to the size required, draw the angel playing the trumpet on to the back of some gold card and cut out. Draw on the features with a black felt-tip pen. Make a bow out of gold crêpe paper and stick it on to the top of the wreath.

5 Now fix the angel to the left-hand side of the wreath.

TREE DECORATIONS

*Good, unusual Christmas decorations are often hard to find. If you want
an alternative to glittery baubles then you may like to make these
decorations from papier mâché, or you could design your own.*

MATERIALS

pencil
tracing paper
thin card
craft knife
small metal jewellery hangers,
one for each decoration
strong clear glue
masking tape
newspaper
diluted PVA (white) glue
fine sandpaper
paintbrush
white paint
pencil
assortment of poster paints
black ink (optional)
non-toxic clear gloss varnish
cord to hang decorations

1 Trace the decoration shapes
from the template, scaling up
to the size required, and transfer
them to the thin card. Cut out each
shape. Stick a hanger on to the back
of each decoration with strong clear
glue, and hold it in place with
masking tape.

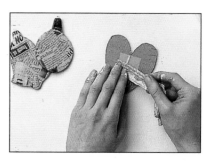

2 Allow the glue to dry for an
hour, and then cover each
decoration with three layers of small,
thin newspaper strips soaked in
diluted PVA (white) glue. Leave to
dry in a warm place overnight.

3 Then sand the dry decorations
lightly with fine sandpaper, and
prime each one with two coats of
white paint.

4 Draw in your design with pencil, and then colour your decorations with poster paints. Define details with black ink, if required. Allow the decorations to dry, and then seal them with two coats of clear gloss varnish. When they are dry, tie a loop of cord to the top of each decoration.

INDEX